THE 21st CENTURY PANDEMIC

Grief and Gifts

"Lest we forget."

Ellie Caldwell

ISBN: 9798861105897
Imprint: Independently published

Production editor: John Vincent Palozzi
Cover art: Google clip art

Caldwell, Ellie,
THE 21st CENTURY PANDEMIC: Grief and Gifts.
 1. Pandemic 2. Sociology. 3. Psychology.

Published in paperback and as an eBook on Amazon Kindle.

DEDICATION

To those who gave: their lives, their dedication, their jobs, their money, their time, and their love, care, attention, and concern for others.

ALSO FROM ELLIE CALDWELL

Available from Southeastern Yearly Meeting and QuakerBooks of FGC: *The Little Quaker Book of De-Clutter*

Available from Amazon, print and eBook:
The Little Quaker Book of Time Mis-Management: How Wasting Time Is Good for the Soul
Your God is Just Wrong: A Continuation of Revelation
This Way In: The Inner Life
Being Church in An Unchurched World
It's Not About Us: The Complications of Caregiving
Give Way: A Lifetime of Surrender
Through the Eyes of Another: Continuing the Conversation on Race

Available as eBooks from Amazon Kindle:
We Don't Have to Get Sick (To Get the Attention We Need)
The Little Quaker Book of Weight Loss
The Little Quaker Book of De-Clutter
Why Our Kids Hate Us (And How They Probably Really Don't)
It's Not About Us: The Complications of Caregiving
Rising Still: Breaking Through the Sadness of Women
Knock, Knock, Who's There? Being Real in an Unreal World & Vice Versa
How to (Somewhat) Disaster-Proof Your Life

CONTENTS

Are we only mistakes, the random combination of chemicals that one day came awake, with no other reason or purpose than chance, whose memory will count for nothing, forgotten once the lights of the universe have gone dark? Is that our story and our fate? Many may believe so. But I say otherwise, for I know we were shaped by an intention older than the stars, brought into consciousness to learn something, to become something, and then to discover just how big life really is.
Bishop Steven Charleston (2/8/23)

The trick, it seems, is to be able to hold both things very close—the gratitude and the misery—and then, with a semblance of faith, to let them fly.
Elizabeth Aquino

FOREWORD

While I live, I remember.
Agnes Vargas

Memory is tricky. We know that. Siblings make each other crazy recalling the same family experience in vastly different detail. We have just survived an international pandemic; none of us will be telling the same story.

We also know that we in the United States have some seriously faulty memory in terms of historical events and news stories during our lifetimes. We ask, "Was I there?" far too often.

We, the citizens of Planet Earth, have spent the last three years living through an international plague, more powerful than flu and more wide-reaching than a periodic or regional outbreak. We're already forgetting our sense of how this began, what it was like in those early days, what we expected, and what took us by surprise. "Flattening the curve" is totally gone from our vocabulary.

Before this becomes another story for the history books and before we begin to pretend it never happened, I'd like to take a look at what has just gone on. Otherwise, faulty memory wins; we learn nothing and just stifle the panic, trauma, and fear. Let's honor the losses, but also let us honor the history we've lived and see what it's taught us as we move forth, as individuals, countries, and a planet.

In this world of 7 billion, our experiences of the last three years differed greatly depending on location, economic status, community, and government leadership. This has been a universal, world-wide, far-reaching explosion of a virus that has shone a huge spotlight on our differences.

Covid 19 or the Coronavirus and its variations have gripped our planet and are probably not done with us yet.

As in any disaster, some people around the world died in far greater numbers: those in poverty, those without medical care, those with no job protection, those with extreme age or medical complications, and those not knowing any better than to wrap themselves in misinformation and lies.

We are a divided people, and politics is only one piece.

I'm writing this in July 2023. Many have not lived to see this date. Although May 11, 2023 marked the end of the "public health emergency" (CDC, 5/12/23), we know people are still getting sick and dying. My son reports that two teachers are out sick at his preschool; he and his wife have had Covid four times.

We in the US have been offered two vaccinations and four boosters; the same is not true around the globe. Cases continue, symptoms seem less serious, but deaths are still occurring where they are reported accurately (which does not include the not-so-enlightened state of Florida). To some extent, "mass immunity" has done its job. We are also told this may become a yearly occurrence like flu, with annual immunization recommended.

The virus may not be completely done with us, but we are done with it. Throughout Covid, large groups of young people continued to party during Spring Break leading to "super spreaders," though the risk is less now. Conferences and live performances are being held again, mostly safely. And we are traveling, as every airport in the world sees an upsurge in travelers tromping through their gates and mostly staying healthy.

We want to dismiss this time. We want to "get back to normal," but I doubt that's ever going to be possible. Or that "normal" ever was.

A conversation in early 2020 with my then 5-year-old granddaughter Reagan spoke of how we felt then: "Gramma, we're being careful at school. It's a virus. But Mom and Dad don't have it, you and Poppa aren't sick, and Eli and I are fine. I think we'll be okay." Wishful thinking of the young that all of us clung to for a long time.

Children want to get back to being children and not worry about germs. Young people want to continue being young and carefree. Having a social life. Learning a trade and building a career, starting a family. Travel lovers want to board cruise lines without worry and shoppers want to shop. "We had a life," we say, and we want it back. Exactly the way it was. Or maybe better. More pizzazz, more highs, more thrills, more cool stuff, more media excitement, more, more, and more.

It's been three years, undergirded by fear, and for much of the time, a sense of not knowing and not being in control. Someone was telling us how to keep ourselves safe, and we needed to listen. And now, here we are. At least, some of us. So what was that all about? A blip on the radar of history? A phenomenal deep-down shift in consciousness? Or something to be put behind us and forgotten as soon as possible?

For these three years, my husband and I have experienced the pandemic from our home in South Florida. We've had all six shots and requested at-home test kits when available. We managed to avoid getting the virus until a trip to Atlanta in October 2022 to see the grandkids. We were both sick for about a week, tested negative, and have gone on with our suburban lives, older but fairly healthy.

We've all experienced three years of being careful. Of staying away from others. Of taking care of ourselves the best we could.

What, I'm now asking, has it all meant? We have learned some serious truths: pandemics are not something world history has erased. We have learned that we, as human beings, are intertwined with each other. Your behavior affects me, the air you breathe is mine, and many factors affect each of us differently, some we control but many we don't.

First, I want to acknowledge the deep losses and sadness. It's been hell to go through these three years. Death and fear. The long-Covid symptoms for many. The debilitating effects. The crushing weight of that grief and sorrow. But also the separations within families and the disillusion about our advanced "modern" age. We are far more vulnerable that we've ever realized.

But then, I want to look at the gifts. Not pretty little gift boxes tied in cheery ribbons, but deep shifts in awareness and learning. Many of these were hard and painfully won. We would rather not know how badly we can function in isolation. Many families will be split forever by the political craziness that has taken hold of some members of our society.

But what do we now know about the world that Covid opened a door to? How have we changed our ideas on what constitutes a "good life"? What values have we rearranged? What has this told us about our lives and how we're spending the time we have here? How will we be living differently from now on?

This is, of course, not a complete examination. I've talked to a number of people and read various articles. But this is mainly put together from my own thoughts and experience.

This writing is, I'm aware, primarily for Americans. Yes, the international pandemic has brought other peoples' realities into our living rooms. On TV, we saw apartment dwellers clapping for health workers in London, and others in Italy listening to music from their courtyards. However, through inability to travel, my personal impressions are here. US, Florida, Palm Beach County. But I suspect they are shared.

We are slowly beginning to walk out of these woods. Look around, see who's still with us. Blink and greet them as the survivors we all are.

We need to see with the new eyes this experience has given us. How is life more valuable? How can we better live in harmony with those we encounter every day or are linked to by blood?

How can we come out of this worldwide pandemic with a deeper sense of purpose and inclusion? With a feeling of unity among people? How have we isolated ourselves from each other for our own survival, but at the same time allowed that to open our eyes and hearts to the lives around us?

Throughout history, many personal and political disasters have happened, probably every day, some we hear of, some we don't. If it's human error, the main players excuse their guilt, lawyer up, and refuse to talk to reporters who are miserably dogged and end up playing the story out as long as they can. But then, the perpetrators wake up some Monday morning, don't see their names in a headline, and realize, "Okay, life's gone on, back to skullduggery and mayhem." There's nothing deader than a dead news story. Who really cares?

But the pandemic of 2020+ doesn't have to be that way. Yes, it'd be great to see it in the rearview mirror, but I suspect it's going to linger. Some have said it may be with us the rest of our lives (for some a longer prospect than others).

Before our plague leaves the stage, how's the world different? How are we changed? What have we learned? I suspect none of us would say it was worth it, but looking for these answers could give this experience some meaning. And I think we'd all love a little of that at this point!

1

GRIEF

My heart is moved by all I cannot save: so much has been destroyed. I have to cast my lot with those who age after age, perversely, with no extraordinary power, reconstitute the world.

Adrienne Rich

The tragedy of the pandemic from 2020+ has been unfathomable: In the US, over a million deaths. Worldwide, the World Health Organization (WHO) reported 767,518,723 confirmed deaths by June 28, 2023. Grandparents in high numbers. Also at one point, more men. People of color. Or those in poor physical health, as well as those with limited access to health care.

Here in the US, the Northwest was a mega-center at first. Then all eyes were glued to New York City, a packed polyglot of a city-state, with close-knit ethnic communities, millions of people barely surviving on a good day and others able to access top medical care, order in groceries, and continue as usual.

Previous plagues have given us images of carts piled high with bodies that townspeople dragged to the curb for pick up. Houses with victims were boarded up and marked with an X. Weeks later, the houses were opened to find not just one dead body, but also everyone else dead too. Similarly, we come out of this plague with images of body bags piled up and bodies stored in meat lockers and walk-in freezers.

Death has touched us. We wept at the first, the second, but after that we kept our grief silent. The losses, so many out in public: Colin Powell, Charley Pride, politicians, actors, musicians, teachers, lawyers, engineers, and even Brad Johnson, aka *The Marlboro Man.* Tragically, one of the first victims was the Chinese doctor, Li Wenliang, who tried to warn the world about Covid in 2019.

If we were squeamish or resisting the reality of death before, now it was in our faces. *Momento mori ("*Remember you must die*").* This is the fate of all. The bell tolls for thee and for me. No one is exempt. From death or from mourning. If you live, you will die. And you will mourn. The following are some noted areas of grief we have lived through.

The Illness Itself. Especially before vaccinations, some people who came down with Covid experienced the worst cases. Ventilators save lives but can be torture. Also isolated patients couldn't be with family members at an extremely emotional and terrifying time of their lives.

Fear was palpable as the virus swept through neighborhoods and worksites. We were all vulnerable; those who could, stayed home and away from the world. "Lockdown" it was called and this time, not to prevent a school shooting, but to keep us all safe.

Long-term Covid. A tiny microscopic virus invaded thousands of bodies and caused symptoms such as respiratory infections, fatigue, fevers, headaches, and more.

The majority of us have taken this seriously, worn masks, and gotten vaccinated as much as possible. Many have still gotten the virus but less severe cases. And when it was over, it was over. But for some people, it wasn't.

For over 36 million people in the US, Covid has lingered and had debilitating effects. Tiredness is probably the most benign, but for older people, it can be a sign of permanent decline. Younger people seemed to get their energy back more easily, but many of us are experiencing some long-term compromised health, autoimmune diseases, or permanent lung or cardiac damage. Treatment and study centers have been set up to support these folks and provide them the continued care they need.

Distance. In most hospitals, visitor restrictions were so extreme, family members weren't able say goodbye to a dying grandparent or parent. Nurses held phones to the ears of patients so the family could say goodbye and "We love you."

Someone invented sleeves in polyurethane sheets so people could put their arms through and hug their grandparents. Hugs, we realized, really are crucial to existence. One psychologist says ten a day for maximum life satisfaction. To go from ten to zero overnight was a shock for all of us. A loving greeting became an elbow bump, not the same.

Division. At a time when every country in the world needed to work together to eradicate this disease and keep their citizens safe, for many people, especially in the US, Covid became divisive and a source of mass anger and frustration.

Some people were opposed to masking. Others were angry about separate lines at the grocery store. Anti-vaxxers felt autoimmune diseases would result from vaccines, but in fact the virus has caused that for many. People made fun of others because they were trying to keep them safe. Covid became an extension of what had led to Donald Trump's election: discontentment and rage, as well as many people feeling that society seemed to be working against them.

Covid peeled back the illusion that we are an educated people. We had seen the results of a high level of ignorance especially during the four years of the "blithering buffoon" as David Brooks (PBS *Nightly News*) called Donald Trump during the 2016 election. In a pandemic, ignorance can be deadly.

Non-Compliance. In the 1950's we lined up in middle school gyms for polio vaccines. 2020 turned out to be a different time. We've seen protests, the questioning of authority, and the rise of "alternative realities" that question science and lack clear thinking.

The compliance of wartime and the 1950's is gone forever and many of us have thought that wasn't so bad. However, "questioning authority" presents itself much differently when rejecting logic, science, and objective facts.

Non-compliance became a stand against everything that seemed to be pitted against the protesters. In some sad cases, this led to their deaths. Many people on the brink of death said, "I wish I'd gotten vaccinated."

Life Cancelled. Many of the ordinary experiences of life were interrupted or cancelled. Graduations. Proms. Weddings had to be scaled down. The fun and escape valve of parties and travel had to be toned down or cancelled. I met people who still hadn't met new grandbabies months after their births.

Like many people, we missed two years of our grandchildren's lives. The years from birth to age five are crucial for establishing bonds and closeness. Covid changed so much. Children can be resilient and we hope we are too, but it's still a loss to be acknowledged.

Social Disruption. Across the globe, we saw how different types of governments dealt with the virus. Brits had pods they were allowed to socialize within. People were not allowed outside their houses except to grocery shop, enforced by British police. Residents could opt to download an app that dinged if they had been exposed to someone who registered as positive for Covid.

All our lives, we have been relieving our restlessness and boredom by socializing with friends, hanging out at our local bars or coffee shops. Or perhaps we'd always indulged in recreational shopping, the addiction of choice for many of us. None of these "relief" opportunities were possible for a while and it took its toll.

For some, quarantine became a time of facing up to the realities of living alone. The sound of only their own voices and perhaps a pet led some to question their life choices.

On the other hand, the challenges of living with others hit us in the face as we established new daily and weekly routines. When people leave the house to work, their annoying habits and work stuff go with them. The constant sounds of other people in the background can test us. Suddenly they were around all the time, humming under their breath and leaving dirty dishes in the sink.

Covid had many challenges, some life threatening, and some just daily annoyances. Most of us told ourselves, "Suck it up, little camper, could be worse." Others weren't so lucky.

Shopping. In the US, shopping was restricted, and Instacart and other shopping services emerged to fill the gap, at least for those who could afford it. Stores established early hours for senior shoppers. The gaps of services for rich and the poor became obvious.

Especially in areas with "food deserts," without aides, friendly neighbors, or church members to provide shopping trips, people were without access to food. In a country as wealthy as ours, it's appalling that corporate profit alone should be the main factor in store locations.

As Dr. Anthony Fauci said, and it bears repeating over and over, "I don't know how to explain to you why you should care about other people." (I discovered that the quote actually originated with Lauren Morrill, a YA fiction writer during the Affordable Care Act debates before DT's election. It could be "borrowed" or could be original to Dr. Fauci, but it's still a good one.)

Senior Risk. Seniors fared even worse in facilities such as nursing homes or hospitals. Staff paid hourly wages were often forced to work even when symptomatic, thus causing widespread illness. Others quit abruptly out of fear for themselves or their families, leaving residents with inadequate care.

Equipment and especially protective gowns and masks were in short supply. In the beginning, buying masks was a novelty; we ordered cute ones from Etsy, providing income for at-home seamstresses. Later we were wiser about better protection and bought N95s.

Some seniors were only willing to peek out the door when family tried to visit; they watched TV, saw too many statistics, and lived in fear. Sadly, some of that fear was justified.

Grief. For a long time many of us could say we knew no one who'd died. The papers were full of obituaries, going to three pages at times in our local *Palm Beach Post*, but we felt exempt. After the second year, though, all of us knew people who'd been sick, died, or lost family members. Grieving as an individual, couple, family, or country are all different. The personal losses began to blur. It seemed as if grief would never leave us, and for many, it hasn't.

The grief was major and overwhelming and so were the social losses. We came together as a planet, but only partially. Some governments treated this like a social ill to use to control their people even further; others floundered to find a balance between safety and trust. We found it was possible to think we couldn't trust anyone.

Spreader Events. A local boss took a business trip to Wuhan in January 2019, held a large office party on his return, and infected most of his employees and their families. Many other mega-spreaders occurred: concerts, cruise ships, and tours, all otherwise known as "Petri dishes" for disease.

For a while, many people had an "it won't happen to me" attitude. Especially healthy young people figured they were exempt. Many found out otherwise, and some were lucky.

Emotional Effects. The emotional toll has been almost as devastating as the physical. With my grandchildren at a park in California, I was chatting with another grandmother with her granddaughter. I said hello to the child and she flinched. Her grandmother said she's fearful of people now, afraid that everyone will make her sick.

Our children, and the rest of us, too, have been terrified by the nightly news and health warnings. We've seen adults unable to prevent the spread of something deadly and the sadness of losing older relatives too early.

The trauma has also been deep-seated, bringing up other ways we feel insecure in the world and how little control we really have over the spread of germs and others' cooperation.

Education. Children are resilient but this has been a powerful and frightening experience for them. Mask wearing and social distancing in schools. Many children at home crouched over laptops, expected to put in long hours of attention, not a normal ability for young children.

For some, such independent studying worked well; for others it meant losing more than a year of learning. We don't know what the long-term effects will be. Some children emerge from dysfunctional homes with lifelong wounds, but others manage to overcome and thrive.

Students lost out on important years of socializing and learning to get along with others. However, many learned new levels of compassion as they tried to keep themselves, their families, and their classmates safe.

Life Events. There was a loss of the momentum of young people's lives as the ordinary markers like graduations and going off to college were postponed or drastically altered.

Weddings were postponed or held outdoors. We couldn't have these markers of our lives, and for some it created great resentment and sadness.

Some young people, especially brides, felt their lives had been ruined. But on the other hand, the possibility of killing your grandmother with a spreader event quickly brought things into perspective.

Fear. We saw the reality of a pandemic played out in many ways in our homes, offices, faith communities, and neighborhoods. We became even more suspicious of each other than we normally are.

Women and children locked at home with abusive spouses saw themselves in daily life-threatening situations. Alcohol and drug use was up, leading to increased violent crime. Although, a remarkable number of people got sober on Zoom AA meetings.

Also, for many stay-at-home parents, this became a stressful time being stuck at home with too many kids and too much chaos. The usual social and recreational outlets were shut down or curtailed. The breaks from full-time parenting were few. Children often paid the price.

Closures. Churches and restaurants closed their doors. Underpaid and overworked staff quit in droves. Many of those jobs and people are permanently gone. Our familiar gathering spots, our casual weekly lunches, or after-work watering holes were shuttered and unavailable as outlets for frustration and isolation.

Some of these have returned, but not all. People got used to sitting with friends in their own backyards. Getting dressed up and going somewhere to socialize began to seem like a lot of work. Some people thought about what they were getting from these gatherings, realized not much, and decided they liked staying home and away from people better.

Housing. Tenants, especially those who could ill afford it, saw huge rent increases. The US government stepped in to offer compassionate relief, but that could only be temporary.

It was as if landlords suddenly panicked over their financial future and collectively decided they weren't gouging their tenants enough. The reputation of landlords in general has been unfairly tarnished for good. But what can renters do? Where can they live?

Also, during these years, interest rates have risen, derailing many young people's plans to purchase homes. Others have felt a serious pinch as they squeezed out even more for banks and home sellers.

In a country where each city has dozens of abandoned homes available for rehab and housing of vets, single moms, and the homeless, it seems we aren't able to imagine this possibility and expect someone else to perform the miracle.

Travel Ban. We all experienced the loss of being able to travel. Throughout our adult lives, we've blithely circled the globe with our love of travel. For many, travel had been a kind of safety valve for the boredom of ordinary life.

It became apparent, though, that our casual flitting about the globe was actually a contributing factor in spreading germs. Travel is supposed to enlighten and spread universal understanding, but the exposure it offers can also be deadly.

Travel writer and tour guide Rick Steves is now back on the road sharing his love of travel. But during lockdown, he admitted how much frustration and loss he was experiencing, just like the rest of us.

Mental Health. Those with mental illnesses such as bipolar, schizophrenia, or depression found themselves severely challenged and isolated. Often their symptoms were exacerbated. They floundered and sought greater support from family, friends, and professionals. Sometimes it was available but often, not.

For many, social distancing required that they accept telemedicine as a safer option. Some felt this was a successful alternative to face-to-face, but others felt even more isolated.

Many people found the technology overwhelming and some didn't even own it. Libraries have become computer learning centers as librarians guide people to use equipment that organizations and social services assume "everyone" has access to.

Loss of Social Circles. We found ourselves stranded without our usual social outlets. Churches, mosques, synagogues, and social clubs were closed and only gradually reopened. Some groups are still struggling to regain their membership. We had lived our lives within the circle of a community that supported us, talked like us, accepted us, and cared for us. That whole network vanished overnight.

Groups have had to rethink how they offer services. Some switched to social media; others changed to 4pm church services or outdoor meetings.

Caution. People became wary of interaction; friendliness was out the window. I've become more careful about casual conversations since the 2016 election, but the pandemic made me doubly cautious.

Most people with possible symptoms isolated themselves to protect others. But many didn't take it seriously. Others might well have been exposed or could be contagious but asymptomatic and refusing to take it seriously. Gone was the sense that we're naturally responsible for others around us. Many people felt rejected and ignored as their needs went unmet.

Losses. People lost family members. They lost jobs. They were evicted. Their support communities closed their doors.

We lost our illusion that people can work together and governments have our best interests in mind.

We lost social connections that had kept us going and the trappings of society that kept fragile lives functioning.

Loss of Control. Along with death and sickness, we've also experienced the reality of living in a world with many dangers out of our control. We couldn't turn our elected officials into responsible leaders overnight. We couldn't make people accept science and see that protecting us is protecting them. We felt a deep disillusion about life in general: what we thought was progress might only be recycled courses of history.

We couldn't control very much, not a bad lesson in life. But generally not one as dangerous as this. Taking care of yourself, being healthy, isolating—all that could mean nothing if you had one encounter with a contagious person.

Distraction. At a time in history when global warming is real, an environmental catastrophe, and wise people are calling for the end of fossil fuels, the pandemic distracted us from whatever climate healing momentum had begun. It felt like a time when everything was put on hold and we just waited until the germs had passed. We'd see who was left and get back to work on the crises of our time.

Climate change, refugees, nuclear weapons, totalitarianism, famine, homelessness, addiction, immigration, the list is endless, as, we could say, it always seems to have been.

Now, in the summer of 2023, the distraction continues: pronouns, trans kids, banning books, and drag queens. We've just come out of a pandemic, a modern day plague, for crying out loud, and instead of getting back to the work of creating a sustainable, peaceful world, we're thrown this malarkey. As a character in Elly Griffith's novels is fond of saying, "Jesus wept."

Disillusion. Society works when we, the general public, feel generally congenial towards each other. We at least minimally trust others to be basically considerate and reasonable, okay people to live next door to and work with. The pandemic has shown us that the "I'll get mine, to heck with you" attitude is alive and well. Maybe, we're thinking, nobody really cares about us at all? Could we really be so wrong about the human race?

One of the first indications was the empty shelves of toilet paper. Such an ordinary and crucial item that people were frightened of running out of. Since then it's been cat food, eggs, certain canned goods, and this week, I heard of a baking powder shortage in London. We imagine people's ancient bomb shelters in their backyards filled with all these random items.

"If there're two, I take only one, so someone else can have one." "If it's two for the price of one, and only two are left, I don't take it because someone else may need it more than I do." Such statements seem absurd and unheard of in our current atmosphere.

We didn't know people were so selfish. So insular. We didn't realize we probably can't go next door to borrow an egg or a cup of sugar anymore.

So we have devolved. Our civilized nature has unraveled. Me first. My family first. My children first. Me, me, me. Sad.

Perhaps understandable in a scary time. And perhaps something that has crept into our society way before this. In my childhood, people were in and out of each other's homes; now, almost never, at least where I live. We feel this asserts our self-reliance and independence from interfering neighbors. But it can also be fatal, can increase the difficulties of aging, and suggest a serious crumbling of the networks we live within.

Heroic Challenges. In all the human services, we saw heroes stretched to the limit and equipment shortages in hospitals, clinics, and senior living facilities. Protective gowns, gloves, and masks became scarce. Nurses were told to come to work even when symptomatic. Insurance set limits on who received what care. Some medications were only available to a few, but were questionable anyway.

For so many, the pandemic meant focusing on keeping other people safe, although many health workers succumbed.

Aging. Covid highlighted some aspects of aging: focus on what matters and appreciate the present. For many, acceptance of aging came sooner than expected during these three years.

For us survivors, it's been a rather rude awakening: we are vulnerable. But more than that, age is a fact of life, a reality we are all forced to accept sooner or later. During Covid, later became now.

After years of being friends with seniors and the younger one in a position to help, suddenly it has become us. We are it. We appreciate an arm to hold onto to cross the street. We board buses carefully. We try to stifle spontaneity in favor of well-thought-out plans for simple activities such as tidying the kitchen or taking a bath.

Age creeps up on us and then it's an everyday experience. How has the last three years made that any different from how life is anyway? This time has made us more conscious of mortality, physical decline, and what it is to be a human with a limited lifespan.

Many people would say this isn't a bad lesson to learn, but it's seemed accelerated and dumped on us all at once. Inevitable, but this has evaporated some of the procrastination.

Changes. Our lives, in many ways, will never be the same. We hate to admit it or shirk at being that dramatic. Maybe I won't continue to wipe down groceries, but I will forever wash my hands after an errand anywhere. I will, at least for the time being, always have a mask in my purse.

We will always worry about older family members in senior facilities. Many of us will always be slightly uncomfortable around large numbers of people.

Economic Cost. Each country in quarantine realized within a short time that an extended period of unemployment and lack of buying/selling was going to have serious effects. People staying home and not working or buying wasn't good for any GNP. In a rush to combat economic slowdown, lives were endangered and some people simply refused to return to their jobs. Often we heard, "It isn't worth it, what they're paying me."

Many small businesses went under since they couldn't absorb the losses large corporate chain stores could. Now three years in, even many large stores like Bed, Bath, and Beyond are going out of business.

At first, corporations shuddered at the economic downturn and wondered if sales would be changed forever. Then, the realization hit: on-line shopping was not only not dead but had flourished and has continued to grow. Malls have been hit hard; many are desperately trying to restructure themselves, and others have become housing for the homeless or office buildings.

Staying home was fine for a few weeks or months, but governments could hardly allow the economy to stall much longer. Our employment and engagement in buying and selling create an economy that works fairly well. People make things and get paid, someone else sells, and usually someone at the top does very well. Note: With all this economic slowdown, weren't you surprised to see how well most of the major corporations have done in the past three years?

Realities. We have been touched by the fickle and fatal finger of history. In our antiseptic and climatically sealed homes in middle-class US, many of us thought we were exempt. Plagues happened in history or at least on the other side of the world. We thought our good diets, exercise programs, positive affirmations, clean living, and efforts to live a good and meaningful life would somehow protect us from the worst. We were wrong. No one is exempt.

Suffering and struggle come to all. And now we've been convinced. This ought to open our eyes and expand our empathy for those suffering around the globe. It could. If it does is yet to be seen.

Vulnerability. Last of all, I want to talk about the lesson in vulnerability of this experience. Most of us in the US have not lived with this sense of vulnerability in our daily lives, in our homes, at work, or in our communities. Yes, daily news and certain TV channels try to convince us that "they" or "something" is out to get us, but most of that can be shrugged off as lies. But Covid brought home to us the reality of our vulnerability in the world.

Throughout our lives, but especially during an international health crisis, we're all vulnerable to the compliance of those around us. Have they been vaccinated? Are they masking?

When will people accept the compassionate belief that we naturally take actions that protect those around us? So many saw masking as an infringement on their liberties. It's as if they'd never lost the two-year-old voice screaming, "You aren't the boss of me!"

We encountered vulnerability in terms of the people we interact with daily or share a home with. Our daughter could have picked up Covid germs from classmates. Our spouses could at work. For a long time, we knew little how it was spread. Exposure could mean contagion and that could happen with anyone. Someone could have sneezed ten seconds before we walked into a grocery store or an elevator.

Around the world, we realized how vulnerable we are in terms of our national leaders. In the US we had a president who in 2018 dismantled the National Security Council directorate at the White House "charged with preparing for when, not if, another pandemic would hit the nation" (APNews 3/14/20). The White House was incapable of assigning leaders to committees or disseminating factual information. Lives were lost while the administration floundered. The same happened in Florida in July 2021 when Gov. DeSantis issued an Executive Order lifting the mask mandate for schools.

In many other countries, national budgets were not sufficient to have adequate disease prevention programs. We have dozens of countries with high levels of natural resources whose leaders are more interested in owning the most Mercedes in the country than in providing health and well being for their citizens.

Since the increased popularity of international travel in the last 50 years, we have all become vulnerable to any bug anywhere that can walk on a plane or sail on a cruise. We have blithely filled our calendars with trips and spent hours on planes and in busy airports without a thought. When we travel overseas, we are all exposed to germs that have never been seen in our country, every one of them thrilled to arrive and propagate like crazy with no natural enemy.

We are also vulnerable to the least educated or least informed among us. A good education doesn't guarantee common sense, good living skills, or a compassionate heart, but it usually does churn out people able to think for themselves, call out BS when they see it, and have some ability to discern false from true.

We are vulnerable in ways we aren't even aware of. The shop that services our car. The mall hangouts where many people spend a huge chunk of their lives enclosed in temperature-controlled spaces with people they know nothing about. Or medical offices which are always full of people with physical challenges.

Disease and pandemics especially can make us paranoid. Or at the very least, ought to make us aware. With whom are we spending our time? Breathing the same air? Who's sharing our seat on the streetcar or in the checkout line behind us at Wawa? We may, possibly, continue some of this wariness and become more careful, but I'm already noticing a desire in all of us to dispense with masks and stroll where we feel like. That seems to mean freedom in 2023.

The panic of previous generations wasn't evident. There were no bells on Covid patients like the lepers exiled to islands or colonies. People got sick in the middle of us, for the most part quarantined or took care of themselves, but that was impossible to do perfectly.

How long does grief last? Does it ever retire or take a day off? Yes, there are grief counselors, books of advice, and videos we can watch. We've all been instructed in the five stages of grief, and we are wiser, we hope, in responding lovingly to friends. We know to reject the platitudes and easy answers.

The only honest answer, it seems, is that there is no answer. Life goes on. Loss and death are a part of life, although seldom in such a continuous assault as a pandemic. We've had to learn to live with something unbearable. This experience has been similar to living through two World Wars for our parents and grandparents. In unbearable circumstances, they survived, just barely, and some didn't. And life went on. No different for some, but irrevocably changed for others.

Grieving takes as long as it takes. And in some ways, it never goes away. It lessens, daily life becomes more bearable, but its touch on our hearts remains.

But also, we have learned something: this is, after all, life. We die. A friend said this week that there's a big difference between people in the UK and people in the US: the Brits know death. Now we all do.

You get caught into things, she thought.
What can you do?
It isn't what you want to do,
it's what life wants to do.
Susan Glaspell, *The Morning is Near Us*

FUNERAL BLUES

Stop all the clocks, cut off the telephone,
Prevent the dog from barking with a juicy bone,
Silence the pianos and with muffled drum
Bring out the coffin, let the mourners come.

Let aeroplanes circle moaning overhead
Scribbling on the sky the message 'He is Dead'.
Put crepe bows round the white necks of the public doves,
Let the traffic policemen wear black cotton gloves.

He was my North, my South, my East and West,
My working week and my Sunday rest,
My noon, my midnight, my talk, my song;
I thought that love would last forever: I was wrong.

The stars are not wanted now; put out every one,
Pack up the moon and dismantle the sun,
Pour away the ocean and sweep up the wood;
For nothing now can ever come to any good.
W. H. Auden

Have you noticed how most of the talk about the coronavirus treats it as a special problem that we must address so we can get back to normal? No recognition that this pandemic is related to an economy requiring endless growth (which means agriculture and mining push into habitats where only animals live and thus the microbe jumps from bats to humans). No recognition that this pandemic reveals boldly the deadly dangers of endless economic growth on our limited planet (though 10% are skilled at using more than their share, leaving the rest to fend with less than their share). No recognition that the poverty created by the endless growth economy makes so many people highly vulnerable to all its fallouts, and, of course, we're all connected, so what the most vulnerable contract spreads. This is not a special problem to be fixed so we can get back to endless growth economics. That economy is faltering terribly, unable to deliver urgent healthcare needs or an economic base for everyone when they can't work. Much more to think about.

Lee Van Hamm (4/2020)

2

GIFTS

To love. To be loved. … To seek joy in the saddest places. To pursue beauty to its lair. To never simplify what is complicated or complicate what is simple. To respect strength, never power. Above all, to watch. To try and understand. To never look away. And never, never to forget.
Arundhati Roy

In the face of so much loss and disillusion, it feels frivolous to talk about there being anything like a "gift" about these three years. Disease, isolation, suffering, and tragedy have taken their toll. But I still hear people referring to something from these three years that sounds very close to positive, learning, and even gift.

We don't want to forget this time. So many of the pages of the history we live through are swept aside, and we become people who say to each other, "That wasn't a nice time. Let's not talk about it." I think that might've been our grandparents' attitudes about the Spanish flu of February 1918-April 1920, the Depression, and the two World Wars. Maybe other families had such discussions around the dinner table, but ours certainly did not. "Why dwell on those years?" they said. "Why stay in that negative place?"

Yet, if we can stay in those memories a little longer, perhaps we can see some parts that gave us greater understanding. Perhaps there were life lessons, empathy, growth, or insights we couldn't have learned any other way.

Clear the Room. My friend Lisa has spoken of the pandemic of 2020+ as a time when we "cleared the room." We had to stay home. Sit with ourselves, the "whiney little babies" we are. We got rid of all the hangers-on, the folks we really couldn't stand but couldn't tell to go home. Got rid of the narcissists and egocentric drama queens.

In addition, though, we got rid of all our lovely distractions that kept up the illusion that our lives had meaning and we really were okay. We had to sit by ourselves for awhile, as if the Universe had said, "Go to your room, think about what you've done, and don't come out until you can be civilized!"

After that clearing out, we were able to be more discerning: Who and what do I want to let back in?

One woman told me she lost three friends during the pandemic. "They're still alive, I'm glad about that, but I found I didn't want to associate with them too frequently and gradually the connection petered out. Their phone calls had been all about them with little interest in my challenges. Or they picked arguments and I had no interest in engaging anymore. Better things to do with my time. Another friend was always late for our scheduled phone calls and never let me know. I thought, enough already.

"I struggled with what to say, didn't want to hurt feelings or get attacked. But apparently I did it firmly but kindly enough so they're gone, but they still speak positively about me to other people. It was effective, but kind of wussy. A direct confrontation might have taught them something about themselves but on the other hand, I doubt they're really capable of that. Alas!"

This also became a time to eliminate activities or involvements that no longer had meaning for us once we had the time to look at them. We were forced to eliminate mindless socializing or drinking parties that could possibly be deadly spreader events. A pause like that allows us to consider where our time and lives are going, who we're spending our time with, and what really gives us a sense of meaning and satisfaction.

Time. We had time: To write the books we'd always said we were going to write. Practice the musical instruments we never had time for. Putter around our gardens. Discover the healing experience of leaning into a tree once in a while.

Some people said, "I always said I'd practice the piano if I had more time and now I realize that wasn't the problem." But many took advantage of the time and allowed themselves to engage in activities they enjoyed but had never had time for.

There also seemed to be a shift in how time passed. A week seemed to fly by. Oh, it's Sunday again? I'm not sure if this was positive or negative—hours and whole days just slipping through our fingers. To some extent, it gave us a sense of appreciating the passage of time, although also a sense of sadness. Time's passing, "Get on with it!" (A quote I picked up from Goldie Hawn years ago and have on my workroom bulletin board).

Redefining Work. Employers discovered that people could be productive at home as well as in a cubicle 45 miles away. This required trust from employers, and some found they really weren't capable of that. This also suggests that they might not have been the best bosses in the world anyway if they couldn't trust the people they hired.

Employees found they were able to be more a part of their families. They could be present with their children throughout the day, not just dinner and bedtime, not the best time to get to know your children.

Couples saw every day what the other does. If one partner had been working outside the home, they were able to note the stay-at-home partner's care of children and home, and learn what they'd been dealing with for decades or more.

The stay-at-home partner got to see the dedication of the partner sticking to a work schedule and concentrating on a project even in the frequent chaos of the home. Couples balanced work/home/kids in different ways and some found they liked it better.

"Work" became more a part of daily life, within a balance, not something removed and distant.

With remote working, the wear and tear on cars decreased. Use of gasoline declined. Fewer people had to dress up in work attire to work at home or participate in Zoom calls, with a few embarrassing moments when pajamas or lack of pants was revealed.

Essential Workers. We quickly saw whose work is "essential." Health workers first and foremost.

Infectious disease experts. Doctors, RNs, CNAs, ambulance drivers, and all the other employees of the medical world.

In addition, we saw how essential food service workers are. Those who grow food, run restaurants, wait table, and those behind the scenes. Delivery folks brought food to shut-ins, which were all of us for part of that time. Or at least those who could afford it or qualified for meals on wheels.

Other essential workers were those in the transportation industry in general. Car and truck mechanics. Truck drivers with supply line control. Plus government workers sending out masks, test kits, and following through on government aid.

School teachers took on super-hero status as they navigated on-line classes with in-person, trying to protect themselves and their students. Mask mandates were different in each school, state, or county. Some parents complied and some children were flexible, but overall it's been fairly disastrous for learning.

Many teachers reconsidered what they'd chosen for a life-time career. Was it really worth it when so many new demands were added daily? A large number have left school systems in the last three years.

Now, after all these challenges, teachers are putting up with state and county demands for less "woke" curriculum as school board members and parents demand sanitized teaching of history and culture. The education of our young is never without challenges, either from legislators, school systems, world-wide pandemics, parents, and the little darlings themselves. But today seems a particularly tough time.

News media people became more and more valued for the reports they transmitted during those dark days. They kept information flowing, protected the people they worked with, and put themselves second, often succumbing to Covid themselves.

Out of this struggle and life threat for many has come, we hope, an appreciation for those who have always put their lives on the line for us in their jobs, put their work first, and been there in good times and bad.

Essence. Our lives got down to essence. What do you want to be doing with your life? This was a time to shift our focus. We found the motivation and strength to lop off unreasonable expectations or unnecessary responsibilities.

Maybe we'd been involved in local politics for years but realized we were going through the motions and not feeling much satisfaction, so walked away when more than two people at a distance in a room could be life threatening.

One friend realized he didn't really enjoy golf, something he'd done nearly every Saturday of his adult life. Another friend decided she was sick of knitting and decided to teach herself embroidery. We had time to sit and think, ponder, or "hold in our hearts," and some of us found we'd grown away from activities we'd kept on our calendars out of expectation and not passion.

These three years have been a time to reassess our lives, redirect our energy, or realign with our true values.

Aging. Many of us came to acknowledge the reality of aging. As my friend Sharon, age 73, said, "Before Covid, I think I basically felt like 12 in my head. Age limitations had so far been few, a little osteoarthritis, arms getting shorter/print getting smaller, but mostly I was able to do what I've been doing for decades. Maybe this wasn't a 'gift,' but more like a needed shift and acceptance. I really don't have half a century left. How am I going to spend the rest of my days? Where is the meaning and purpose I need?"

For some people, it felt like a time of facing life on life's terms and accepting adulthood. Many slipped into maturity, accepting reality and realizing the importance of purpose no matter their age.

Books. We had lots of time for reading and many of us discovered new authors and explored worlds we knew nothing about. Through social media, we found ways to share our new finds and discover new authors.

The first year of the pandemic, I sat on the back porch every night after supper reading a section of Robin Wall Kimmerer's *Braiding Sweetgrass*. Then I read *Sand Talk* by Tyson Yunkaporta that my friend Sandra in Australia had given me. For several months I explored indigenous writing from different parts of the planet; so much resonates with us, and it's teaching we need.

One friend discovered a new mystery writer and spent many weeks solving crimes and enjoying the British country scene. She said, "I can't imagine how people are surviving this who don't love reading!"

Other Explorations. This became an opportunity for people to explore spiritual or intellectual ideas they'd never had time for. My friend Martha watched Sufi videos. Virginia explored the Feldenkrais method, something she'd always found fascinating. It increased her awareness of muscles and movement, but she ended up concluding that trying to do the exercises by Zoom on an iPad was too challenging.

Friends dragged out cookbooks or explored the internet for new recipes and flavors they missed. Couldn't eat at your favorite Indian restaurant? Figure out how to make it yourself. Sour dough starters reached high popularity.

Friends who missed travel discovered Rick Steves' videos and NHK (Japanese TV) shows on travel and culture.

As my friend Mariah said, "The world is really a fascinating place with lots to explore. Our tech devices can keep us sheltered in a little screen world if we're not careful. Sure, I enjoy it some, but I enjoy a walk in the woods with a new friend more."

Redesigned Shopping. Besides grocery deliveries, many of us increased our on-line shopping, keeping out of box stores and crowded malls. This probably protected us, but also decreased the amount of "recreational" spending we indulged in.

Many of us found our discretionary funds increased by Covid when we didn't go out much and didn't need new clothes too often. One friend said, "I look decent when I'm out, but when I come home, I ditch the bra and hang out in about three things. I try to appear okay in public but kind of look like a homeless person at home. Comfortable though!"

Repair, Recycle, Reuse. We've heard the eco-slogans for years, but now we had an even greater opportunity to participate. Sewing machines came out and clothing repairs became more popular. When you can't buy new, keep the old going as long as possible.

In the process, we discovered half-finished handicraft projects; a good time to finish them up! Or pass on to someone who might.

Some of us took a look at our garages or store rooms and asked, "Why am I holding onto that?" All those "just in case" spare parts we can't even remember what they go to or the original item was thrown out years ago. Donations, recycling, or trash.

A few new habits took hold as we remembered how to darn socks and figured out how to make a new cord for pants.

Many people became more conscientious about recycling and better informed about what exactly could be recycled and what couldn't. Others got interested in living a "zero waste" life, consciously buying recyclable goods or not buying any single-use plastic items.

Decluttering. Spending so much time in our homes made us want more nurturing and less cluttered environments. Thrift stores and charity shops were slightly overwhelmed with cast offs but dealt with the riches.

Out went extra *tchotchkes* that meant nothing to us anymore or we never really liked. Clothing in the back of the closet we hadn't worn in years, too big, too small, or too ugly. Shoes that look cute but hurt like heck. Out-of-date clothing. Worn-out sheets and towels. Fewer, less, none.

Most towns have several choices for donations. In Palm Beach County, we have high-end Hospice Thrift Shops, Goodwill, and a Resource Depot, for specific items teachers and kids can use for school projects. Their website lists donatable items and appointments are necessary. One item is oatmeal containers of which we have had a windfall during the last couple years.

A home should be a nurturing environment, where we feel safe, can relax, and aren't always thinking, "Oh, I should get to that." A room without clutter becomes a more pleasant place to spend our lives.

The same goes for a back yard: comfortable and relaxing. But for many of us that becomes another "ought" and maybe accepting "as is" and getting to it as we can is the better choice. A shift in thinking can change everything!

Home Repairs. Another side consequence of spending so much time at home: we realized home repairs were not going to fix themselves and the small plumbing project we thought we could fix ourselves wasn't going to happen.

Also with eating out less, buying less gas, and shopping less, we could afford repairs we'd been putting off. Or repairs we were never going to get to and didn't really have the skills to consider.

Repairmen reported they were busier than ever. People renovated bathrooms, redid landscaping, and refinished garages.

As with decluttering, small repairs enhanced our environments and made it more pleasant to spend time within our four walls.

Friendships. One woman told me she had become friends with two women in her neighborhood at the beginning of the pandemic: "We'd check on each other from time to time on the phone and got to know more of the details of each other's lives. About a year in, someone suggested we walk in the mornings and now that's what we do about three days a week. We meet at one woman's house who's about half way, and then we walk—and talk of course—for about an hour. It's made a huge difference to our sense of not being so isolated during this time. And to think, I never would have started this healthy routine of walking on my own!"

Limited in our ability to meet friends for lunch or visit in each other's homes, we found other ways to make connections. Sometimes we found ourselves getting to know people we'd not been much aware of though they lived nearby. Our worlds contracted in so many ways that new friendships were a breath of hope and the possibility of a different future.

Technology. Many of us discovered the joy of connection without leaving our homes through technology. FaceTime, Skype, Zoom, WhatsApp and others have enabled friendships around the globe. Instead of slumping into "poor me" and feeling alone, many singles have reached out across the miles to share their lives.

At first many of us were skeptical. Talking to others on a screen seemed intrusive and artificial. How can our contact possibly have as much depth as one-on-one? It seemed as if we were permitting technology to impinge too far into our lives and our connections to others. Also, how can I stand to look at myself on a screen for an hour?

But with time, self-consciousness gave way to curiosity. We could still look into people's eyes and read body language, certainly more than when talking by phone. We could still listen and be listened to, and out of that grew meaningful connections.

Many church services were forced to close in the beginning of Covid but after a while, some purchased Zoom equipment and took to the air. Others utilized YouTube, taping church services that parishioners could view later in the week not just at the official 11am Sunday time slot.

When on-line services gradually morphed into hybrid gatherings (how our vocabulary has been enhanced!), some people took to it gratefully. Those at a distance, those with physical or mental challenges, or those with immune deficiencies were now able to be part of worship.

For some, this progress has not come easily. Worshiping in the presence of technology seemed unnatural and uncomfortable to them. Some felt there was a desecration of sacred space. Another person said about our silent Quaker worship, "What's the difference? I have my eyes closed in the silence anyway."

I suspect a similar horror about technology was voiced in the early 20th Century when electricity was brought into churches, synagogues, temples, mosques, and meetinghouses. I can imagine early Quakers saying, "We carry the Light within! There's no need for godless electric lighting!" Or for that matter, in Florida, the addition of carpeting instead of rush matting or air conditioning itself. There will be change; life is change.

Yes, it won't all be to everyone's liking, but it will happen. Overall, especially when change comes about from the Quaker "sense of the Meeting" decision-making, it might be the wiser choice to decide how one can live with something which is a positive change for everyone else. Plus, if we still suffer from self-consciousness, there's always the "hide self-view" button.

Human contact came to depend on technology, which we reluctantly accepted as the best we could do and then embraced it for the meaningful interaction it provided.

Although grandparents and other relatives were separated, social media launched us into virtual families.

Sometimes families were just too chaotic to use it much. But for many, it became a lifeline to keep in touch.

Friends found themselves in more frequent contact with each other through WhatsApp, Skype, Zoom, and FaceTime. One friend said, "My cousins and I had weekly contact during Covid. I hope it keeps up though everyone's getting busy again." Many Zoom communities grew and have created new friendships across the globe.

Many faith or social communities found continuing closeness from technology such as group chats or texting. As one member said, "We're not just Sunday friends anymore." Members texted each other off and on during the week and began to feel a greater connection to friends' daily lives. Just a "How's it going?" on a dreary and lonely Wednesday morning gave people a lift. We felt warmed by being thought of and were gratified that someone reached out.

New Routines. At first, many of us thought Covid would last a few weeks: "It'll be worst in the second week of April," a local doctor said in March 2020. But as time dragged on, we realized we were in for the long haul, something we aren't used to in our lives.

What set in for the first few weeks was some depression, a little shock, disbelief, fury, and a bleak sense of being a walking target and not knowing what to do about it except stay home and be careful.

Gradually some new habits crept in. *WORDLE* was invented, shared, then bought by the *New York Times* in January 2022 (*NYT,* 1/31/22), and became a standard morning activity for millions. The same with the famous *Spelling Bee* and various daily crossword puzzles. These became the "new normal" as we realized the need to have some kind of structure and even ritual in our days. Some mental calisthenics first thing in the morning!

Of course these games also became one more source of bragging on Facebook, but we've found it doesn't take much: food, cute babies, and adorable pets of all types. In fact, it's interesting that Facebook is now vacated by most people under age 40 and anyone who considers themselves "cool." (But of course, they don't know "the 70's rock.")

That means Facebook's evolved into a community (of sorts) for people with similar interests, e.g., health food, spirituality, nature, exercise, reading, or crafts, at least that's what my feed serves up. I seldom hear a peep from anyone I disagree with. It's got a small sense of community, maybe like a local coffee shop minus the chance of exposure to Covid.

For many, social media transformed this lonely, frightened time into connections we might not have nurtured much in the past. Not the same as face-to-face, but at least an antidote for loneliness or hanging out with the mostly unsympathetic cats.

But I'm also never able to forget that there are controls behind the Facebook Wizard and algorithms I have little awareness of (not good). For what I like it for, I accept the negatives. And scrolling through almost always serves up a lovely nap on Sunday afternoons after Quaker Meeting. Best sleeping pill in the world!

Of course new routines also meant planning grocery shopping around senior hours, limiting trips out, and discovering the necessity each day to have contact with the real world. We were isolated, some more than others, but we found ways to connect even when miles apart and also keep all of us safe.

Grief "Gifts." Along with grief came gifts out of sadness. My friend Joel spoke of a cruise that was cancelled, but then the same week, his mother became sick and was hospitalized. She responded to medical care, but it was apparent she was failing. Because of Covid, only one visitor was allowed at a time, and if Joel left, he wasn't able to return. When she was moved to hospice, two visitors were allowed for two hours at a time, and Joel's sister and her husband were able to visit. Covid had cancelled his cruise, he was present for his mother's death, but it made being present much more complicated.

So, there have been a few "gifts" despite this international tragedy. Our lives have been enhanced in various ways, some temporary, and some have seemed to last. We have gained a sense of connection to people around the world. We've seen them clapping for health professionals and listened to their stories of bereavement and loss. We know more than ever that "they is us."

We've also been able to partake in a universal "pause." Our lives and our livelihoods have been on hold.

We've gotten to question the direction and values of how we had been living.

Even with much to feel frustrated, angry, and resentful about, many kept up their basically good-natured personalities and found something each day to help them keep going or maybe even laugh out loud.

Most of all, I think we've gained a new appreciation for our families and friends. We've realized how lucky we are to have people it's possible to quarantine with and manage to still love. How fortunate to have people who call frequently to check on us.

Also, how wonderful if we already had a love of reading, an enjoyment of old movies, a yard to putter around in, or an ability to do odd jobs around our house.

Those of us considered "baby boomers" have grown up in a particularly cynical time. We started out all love and peace in the Sixties, committed to living out our values and saving the world, if possible by the time we were age 30. Then came the years of Watergate, Vietnam, and increased media scrutiny. We now know more than we want to about every misstep of every famous person and especially our leaders in Washington. There was much talk of "draining the swamp," which hardly occurred, but no mention at all of the muck you get when the pretty water's gone. Good for growing water lilies but not much else, and it stinks.

We've become a culture of expecting little, making fun easily, deriding too much love and peace, and accepting a world of the smart aleck and cynic. When you've already imagined the worse that could happen, you shrug off everything.

Now we've had three years to re-examine that "oh-so-cool" stance. Suddenly we've come face to face with the facts: it's a gift to have a grandmother you can cherish. Great fortune to have dear friends you can share blunders and achievements with. Someone who gifts you with a thoughtful note—a real, snail mail note— is an angel indeed.

Most of all, perhaps we've been given a glimpse of how much it means to have a sense of purpose in our lives, especially in our later years. Those of us lucky to make it beyond age 60, unheard of not that long ago, have seen quite clearly what enriches our days and continues to bring love and laughter.

For many people, this has become a time of learning to live better. Learning to appreciate more. Learning to let the positive in. And cherish the simple, yet complex, joys of the privilege of life.

3

STORIES

Our souls are hungry for meaning, the sense that we figured out how to live so that our lives matter so the world will be at least a little bit different for our having passed through it.
Rabbi Harold Kushner

Thecla Geraghty, London, UK: Originally from the US, Thecla has been living in London since 1990, involved in Quaker organizations. I met her a few months into the pandemic through a Quaker-based Zoom group out of Nashville, Tennessee, and we've kept in touch through Zoom and texting.

"For me, there were lots of positives in remote communication such as FaceTime, Skype, and Zoom. Especially helpful for anyone who's agoraphobic, shy, or introverted. We could engage with more people but with less stress. People can feel as if there's nothing 'wrong' with them when meeting on Zoom and know others feel the same. There was separation and loneliness during the pandemic, but with Zoom, we felt connected and seen."

In the first weeks of lockdown, she had three Zoom events. She was interacting with more people but not feeling exhausted. "All of us had to overcome some self-consciousness in the beginning, but gradually most people found it non-threatening." She spent some time figuring out the settings and updated her camera and lighting to make it feel "homier."

Brits felt they were "doing the right thing" and there was a positive sense of helping each other. "If you're in a shipwreck," she said, "most people will be nice."

At her local market, Thecla often thanked the clerks for coming to work that day. When she later asked for eggs, the grocer gave her the dozen he'd put aside for his family. There was a sense that "at least we have each other."

A major concern early on was rising fuel costs. People kept their thermostats as low as possible to economize, hard on older people and those with health challenges.

The changes in shifts at work were good overall with more people working from home. This was actually positive for the environment, families, introverts, and traffic. Although, it required trust between employee and employer; at some work sites, programs were installed to check key strokes on computers to ensure employees were working.

Being single had particular challenges, but so did family life. Without pets, a partner, or children, some people found life difficult. But, really, it wasn't easy for anyone.

Theaters shut down, so there was no income for the employees. The same was true for those in the arts, tourism, or restaurants. Unions helped members continue to have some income, but the pandemic showed clearly the vulnerability of these areas of work.

Some people found they were trusting each other more. Neighbors reached out to help with food or medicine deliveries. People made an effort to check up on each other and help when needed.

The British Quaker study center, Woodbrooke, went completely on line, which offered more time for visiting and getting to know each other before and after Zoom calls. The British Quaker world in general became more accessible, especially for those who are neuro-diverse, have immune issues, lack funds to travel to meetings, or have mobility problems. Many said, "Now I can really live," meaning they were able to interact and be present like other people. Relating on Zoom, many were not stressed by being "out in public."

She suggested, "Perhaps we need some discernment in Quaker Meetings and other faith communities on the use of on-line meetings as we go forward. Zoom seems to work for some groups, but not all. We need to develop hybrid meetings so we can be even more inclusive. Zoom has become an effective way of communicating and creating a faith community."

Ashley Ouellette, Wellington, FL: Ashley is a real estate agent who's lived in Florida for 22 years. She comes from a large family originating in the Lake of the Ozarks, Missouri.

For her, the pandemic was about family and trying to keep her career afloat. She said, "The worst of it was friends and family dying alone in hospitals and hospice.

"My father lived with his children in Missouri (six of nine children still live there), but would visit me for the winter months and was with me in January 2020 when Covid hit. He moved in permanently in May 2020 and died in June 2021 at the age of 90 from cancer. He died quickly but all his children were able to fly in and say goodbye, unlike those who died from Covid alone in the hospital.

"At the same time I became aware of the nature around my home. The bees and butterflies in the bushes were just magical, a place of peace.

"My brother died before the pandemic, but that was the beginning of knowing this peace. When the pandemic came, it made it easier to slip into this understanding of family and nature. I didn't want to miss the good moments, like spending time with my dad each morning getting him ready for the day. It went from a 'job' to a 'joy.'"

She feels we came to a greater global appreciation of each other and our planet, an "awakening experience" shared by others. It was as if all of us were becoming more at one with the rest of the world.

At the beginning, no one knew how long this would last and everyone was urged to stay home. This led to loneliness and separation from work colleagues. Also for many who were paid by the hour, it meant no money coming in for their families.

"In real estate, transactions actually became easier with technology. A sense of trust developed as people relied on others to wire forms and money. At the same time, investors were freaking out and real estate sales were slipping badly."

However, people always need houses so things began to pick up before long. The Paycheck Protection Loans (PPP) from the government were profoundly helpful, and she was able to use her connections and computer skills to help others get the money to survive in their businesses. Everything gradually opened up in terms of business and banking, but also, in some areas, with more opportunities and connections that hadn't existed before the pandemic.

Each day we emerge anew
from the soup of our own chaos.
Hungry for reason and order,
we deny that, like God, perhaps,
we too live on the edge
of trial and error, always
on the brink of possibility,
always moving into the next moment
of clarity and complexity,
the next dawning of day
the next wonder
of darkness and light.
Michael S. Glaser

Praise What Comes

Surprising as unplanned kisses, all you haven't deserved
of days and solitude, your body's immoderate good health
that lets you work in many kinds of weather. Praise
talk with just about anyone. And quiet intervals, books
that are your food and your hunger; nightfall and walks
before sleep. Praising these for practice, perhaps
you will come at last to praise grief and the wrongs
you never intended. At the end there may be no answers
and only a few very simple questions: did I love,
finish my task in the world? Learn at least one
of the many names of God? At the intersections,
the boundaries where one life began and another
ended, the jumping-off places between fear and
possibility, at the ragged edges of pain,
did I catch the smallest glimpse of the holy?

Jeanne Lohmann, *The Light of Invisible Bodies*

4

FINAL THOUGHTS

And once the storm is over, you won't remember how you made it through, how you managed to survive. You won't even be sure, whether the storm is really over. But one thing is certain. When you come out of the storm, you won't be the same person who walked in. That's what this storm's all about.
Haruki Murakami

It is now August of 2023. In May 2023 the CDC announced the pandemic is over. I suspect this is magical thinking on some level; it feels as if Covid could be with us for a while. Just last week a friend in a senior facility told me they're on lockdown again with more than 20 cases of Covid.

Americans are good at passing through history seeing and hearing what we choose with our own binders. We like stories that make us look good and want to do what we want with our lives, with no one telling us how.

Easter just past was a widespread celebration of chocolate and crucifixes, bunnies and bleeding hearts. Driving home that day, I found the traffic in Palm Beach County was overwhelming. Everyone going somewhere, having someone to see, something to buy, something to grill or drink, or just wanting to be out of the house and with other people. The punishment is over, we're free, let the festivities begin.

And yet, now we hear more people have come down with Covid; some are minor cases due to vaccinations, but still it's a presence. Our son and his wife in New Zealand have it again.

So what has it meant? What did we learn?

A few women around the country realized their marriages were a mistake. Or they shouldn't have to put up with so much struggle and abuse.

Some gig workers realized the fragility of their economic situation and worked out a better plan. Or hourly workers realized they were never going to make enough to survive and raise a family so looked around for what else might work better.

Some took early retirement, realizing the opportunity at last to live as they chose for a few years was too good to pass up. For others, perhaps it was a time to evaluate the direction of their lives and come to the conclusion they're worth something more—better pay, sobriety, better family relations, a better living situation, or just a better life in general.

If we're able get something better out of this, it'll feel as if it might have been worth it. Nothing can make up for the deaths, but perhaps each of us can find meaning that comforts and allows us to move on.

I sense it's possible we've learned something about our vulnerability as planetary citizens, but also our interconnectedness. A lab in Wuhan, a canal in Venice, a mountain trail in Peru, an ER in New York City—all of us tied together in a web of humanity. Our polluted rivers are theirs; their cleared forests or lost vegetation is ours.

Maybe we now take life less for granted. We've learned to engage and cherish the time we have with each other. Lavish love on our children and guide them gently. Bow to our teachers, our elders, the medical workers, and all the ones who showed us the way.

We need to learn the demands and requirements of life, but also schedule times of rest and renewal. Each period of our lives sets a pace, and we run the course we're given, holding onto this tiger's tail or at times lying down and napping by its side.

Now, sort of out the other side, we need to wake up and deal with a planet that's taken a beating. As countries, we have set deadlines for renewable energy, but little has been done. We need to eliminate fossil fuels. Build up international renewal energy. Save, recycle, renew, refuse to buy, repair what you can, and appreciate what you have.

There is, as many have said, no "Planet B." A pandemic gets your attention, but it's not a permanent detour. Return now to the work of being human: feed the hungry, clothe the weary, lift up, suffer with, and make another's walk a little easier each day.

We have the assignment; we know the tasks that are ours. Get on with it! Back from the brink, but maybe a little wiser, more compassionate, more empathetic, and more aware. We are all—all—in this together, ever have been, ever will be.

And the people stayed home. And read books, and listened, and rested, and exercised, and made art, and played games, and learned new ways of being, and were still. And listened more deeply. Some meditated, some prayed, some danced. Some met their shadows. And the people began to think differently. And the people healed. And, in the absence of people living in ignorant, dangerous, mindless, and heartless ways, the earth began to heal. And when the danger passed, and the people joined together again, they grieved their losses, and made new choices, and dreamed new images, and created new ways to live and heal the earth fully, as they had been healed.

Kitty O'Meara, *And The People Stayed Home.*

DISCUSSION QUESTIONS

1. What were the most difficult aspects of the Covid Pandemic for you? What made you angry? Despair? Sad?

2. Name some people you lost. Family members and new grandchildren you lost time with. Work disruption. Financial losses.

3. What routines helped you through lock down? What new activities came into your life?

4. How has Covid affected your life going forward? What new behavior do you see continuing? How has your future been changed?

5. What would you recommend to people who are still struggling to get back a semblance of normalcy?

6. What changes in the world have you seen as a result of the pandemic?

7. What was helpful during Covid? What was not?

**Be soft. Do not let the world make you hard. Do not
let the pain make you hate. Do not let the bitterness
steal your sweetness. Take pride that even though
the rest of the world may disagree, you still believe
it to be a beautiful place.**
Iain Thomas, *I Wrote This For You, 2007-17*

**Someone I loved once gave me
a box full of darkness.
It took me years to understand
that this, too, was a gift.**
Mary Oliver, *The Uses of Sorrow*

RESOURCES

1. "Covid Experts Today," *Washington Post,* 3/12/23.

2. "Have We Learned Any Lessons from Covid?" *USA Today,* 4/25/23.

3. Kimmerer, Robin Wall, *Braiding Sweetgrass, 2013.*

4. "Long Covid: Where Are We In 2023?," NIH, *Missouri Medicine*, 3/4/23.

5. Mooallem, Jon, "Three Years into Covid, We Still Don't Know How to Talk about It," *New York Times*, 2/22/23.

6. "Not Every Pandemic Needs Someone to Blame," *NYT,* 5/21/23.

7. "The Covid-19 Pandemic: Is It Really Over?" *PBS*, 7/3/23.

8. "Three Years of Covid-19," American Heart Association, 3/9/23.

9. Yunkaporta, Tyson, *Sand Talk: How Indigenous Thinking Can Save the World, 2019.*

10. "What's Going on With Covid Right Now?" *NYT*, 5/5/23.

ACKNOWLEDGEMENTS

To all those who participated in endless discussions about what the pandemic has meant. Those who shared lunches, car trips, and late-night phone calls passing on their perspective. Appreciation to Thecla Geraghty and Linda Karon for being first readers. Thanks to John Palozzi for continued lay out and publishing skills. Family for putting up with distractions and husband, Gary, for continued tech and emotional support. It is hoped that writing skills grow but it seems computer skills are unlikely to. Gratitude to a world that has come through and the leaders that helped or at least didn't stand in the way.

BIOGRAPHY

Ellie Caldwell is still rocking her 70's although with a little more careful step. She's found learning about chakra balancing and mindfulness quite helpful for one's later years. Mostly still based in South Florida, she and her husband are beginning to rotate between New Zealand where her son Aaron and daughter-in-law Elsa live, and Atlanta, where her daughter Kathleen, son-in-law Josh, and grandkids Eli and Reagan have moved. After a few decades in the tropics, the body adjusts and warmth is appreciated. In such a setting "aging in place" has its pluses, but you never know where people will wander off once the pandemic leaves the radar.